The 7 Choices Series

Seven Choices

Save Your Marriage & Sex Life,
Before it's Too Late...

by

Stephen Openshaw, Ph.D.

I have attempted to give credit to other authors wherever possible. As there are no new ideas, the ideas expressed here are the result of over 40 years of learning and practicing Clinical Psychology, including exposure to countless authors and individuals who shaped me to be the Psychologist that I am today. My apologies to anyone who claims ownership of any of these ideas who was not acknowledged. Any lack of acknowledgement is unintentional. I thank all of you who have helped me to be a better Psychologist and a better human being.

This book is dedicated to Bug, the love of my life,
who loved me so much
she set me free in Hawai'i...

Table of Contents

Too Late...

It's another beautiful day on O'ahu. I'm heading to work on Monday morning, making that amazing drive around Makapu'u, seeing the green hills and the beautiful turquoise water, I am happy. I have no idea, no clue, that my life will change dramatically today. As I look down at Waimanalo and out toward the Marine Corps base, I remember my commitment to that view; I never want to be so jaded or distracted that I don't appreciate how beautiful it is. I turn up the music as I slowly come around the bend and take in the ocean, the craggy green cliffs and the seemingly endless beaches stretching down Waimanalo to Kailua and the Marine Corps base beyond. I feel so fortunate, so lucky to have this opportunity. I have a great new job, embedded in a Marine battalion for a year at a time, counseling and helping Marines and their families with whatever they need to support their success. I drive up to the gate at the base and the Marine guarding the gate checks my ID.

"Good morning lance corporal. How are you today?" I ask.

"Fine, sir. Welcome to Marine Corps Base Hawai'i. You have a nice day."

I am a Clinical Psychologist and practiced in southern California for over 30 years before moving to Hawai'i. I mostly worked with couples, individuals needing help with stress, anxiety or depression, and people with medical concerns related to my work at St. Jude Medical Center in

Fullerton. I also wore a lot of other hats and stayed active in the local community.

I met my wife in 1990 and we had a wonderful life together for over 23 years. Although we were not blessed with children, we had lots of extended family and nieces and nephews. We had lots of friends and a busy social life, and had the opportunity to travel all over the world together, sometimes for as long as a month at a time.

One of our favorite places was Hawai'i. I was hooked on the place because I had been brain-washed by my great aunt Marion about Hawai'i since I was an infant. She had lived there in the 1930's and had a pharmacy in Honolulu. She came back before the war, but I think she left her heart in Hawai'i, and frequently shared that love with me.

I had very little supervision during much of my childhood, but fortunately I had Marion, mostly for months every summer at my grandmother's cabin in the Sierra Nevada mountains. She was an amazing woman. Six feet tall, she never married but kind of adopted me and my brother and told us what was what... in no uncertain terms!

So, I always wanted to live in Hawai'i and eventually my wife and I decided to move to O'ahu. I closed my practice and my wife got a high-powered, high-paying job that allowed her to work from Hawai'i. We sold our house and moved to O'ahu. I eventually landed a job working with the Marines, and if you had asked me, I would have told you I was living the dream.

I come home from work that Monday after that glorious drive feeling happy, clueless, to find a note on the entry table. The note says that my wife has left and is filing for divorce, the marriage is over. My heart pounding, I look around the apartment. This can't be true! But it is. Things are missing. I race to her closet... all of her clothes are gone! No! No! No! I collapse on the sofa and cry like I've never cried before...

It is over after 25 years together. After 23 years of marriage, it is over... I know we've been going through a tough time in our marriage; job changes and her business travel, selling our home and then moving to Hawai'i haven't been easy, especially for her. I've been thinking that we need to talk about it and find a better way to adjust to the changes, but I assumed we would get to it, that we would have the time... We don't; it's too late...

Thinking about it, I can see that we have both withdrawn. We've both been unhappy in the relationship with so much change so fast, so little time together, and we've both been acting out in ways that can be destructive to a marriage. I'm kicking myself because I have the skills to fix things. I am a psychologist and I know what to do, but I didn't do those simple things because I haven't been paying attention. So self-absorbed, wrapped up in my day-to-day life. Well, I'm paying attention now. But now it's too late. And now I won't have the chance to use those skills or the opportunity to work on the marriage. She's gone and has no interest in trying again. My faith and my skills don't matter. It's too late...

How can I get this message across to you? I made a horrible mistake and I want to protect you, save you from making the same or a similar mistake. This book is a warning! I hope that you hear it. I hope that you are paying attention to the love in your life. In this book are seven choices that you can make to keep your love alive, or to find and develop this amazing part of life we call love.

Seven simple choices to save love and keep it alive. Are you paying attention? I really hope that you are! Do not take for granted the riches that already might be in your life... don't let your love wither. This book is a cautionary tale and a gift for you to use or squander. Choose! I say choose to love every day and never forget how fragile and precious it is. Remember that it can disappear in the blink of an eye, and then it might be too late.

There are no bad guys in this story. We were two people trying to do the best we could, but the end of the marriage moved upon us with great stealth. The end of a long marriage is an insidious process, happening small step by small step. It doesn't happen all at once, although it felt that way to me at first. It starts with accepting little things and later big things that, upon reflection, we should never have accepted! A little distance, a little shortness in how we talked sometimes, less concern about looking good for each other and less intimacy were little things that we gradually accepted. It is this increasing distance and a lessening of showing how much you care that you must guard against. If you don't, you might come home one day to find that it is too late...

Love and Madness...

We all want love in our lives because love is the best of all that life has to offer. Love is the best that life has to offer! Whether you are looking for a relationship (even if you are denying wanting one), in a relationship that has lost its spark, or happily *in love* but fearing the loss of love, in this short book are the tools and structure to help you find love and keep it alive. Here you will find the tools to keep your sexual connection alive, vital and passionate.

Love is waiting for you around the corner, in the next conversation, in the next appreciative glance... Only you can make this choice to love and you have to keep on making it, moment by moment, every day. In these pages, you can find out how to love, how to find love and how to keep it alive. The ideas are simple, but we make it complicated, mostly because we are afraid: afraid to get hurt, afraid we are not worthy, afraid we don't know how or will blow it, afraid to look foolish, afraid our love won't be returned, or even *in love* afraid we will lose it...

I would argue that if love does not scare you, you are not risking enough. Courage is going ahead even though you are afraid. Without fear, there is no chance to be courageous. Be courageous! Take a chance on love but make it an informed choice... The seven choices outlined here make love less of a risk or chance, and give you the tools to combat your fears, the skills to find love and keep it alive.

"Being deeply loved by someone gives you strength, while loving someone deeply gives you courage."

- Lao Tzu

If you are in a relationship that once seemed great but has lost something, there are tools here to help get you back on track, tools you can use! Let me give you a head start, a shove in the right direction for those of you who feel that love has lost its spark in your current committed relationship.

I often suggest this to couples I see who seem to be doing well overall, who still like each other but have withdrawn some. I would say that there are probably a hundred things you each could do to make your marriage better that you already know how to do, that you don't need a psychologist to tell you to do. You are not doing them because you are angry, or lazy, or competitive, or you want the other person to do it first. Get up off your lazy you-know-what and do these things!

If you are willing to do at least some of those things, make them count! Do the things that you know will make a difference. If you listen to your partner's complaints, you will discover a wealth of clues about what to do! Maybe you just need to talk nicer to each other or show greater patience. Maybe you just need to help out more around the house. Maybe you just need to focus on your partner a little each day or take them out for a good time more frequently. Listen to him or her and just do it!

Sometimes I joke to couples, "What if I gave you a million dollars to get along perfectly for the next 24 hours? Could you do it?"

"Of course we can!" they chime.

Well, isn't a happy and harmonious marriage worth a million dollars? Be nicer to each other and pitch in without being asked! (More on this in a later chapter.)

It is a peculiar fact that anxiety (fear) and excitement are physiologically identical. We experience them differently because of the difference in context and perspective. Love is the best that life has to offer and it should be exciting and scary! Of course, love can't be that exciting all the time, but you can continue to find those exciting moments even if you've been married for 50 years!

This is the secret everyone is looking for, and so few seem to have found, and it's waiting for you... on the pages that follow. Choose! If you are willing to take the leap, you will discover that it really is a matter of one step at a time and not such a scary leap. The scary part is opening your heart to another person and risking love, caring about being accepted and loved, risking rejection.

I can't help drifting back into the past, thinking about what I have lost... Oh, we were in love! I believe it is important to have a lot in common, and we did. We traveled all over the world and we traveled well together. I was always the romantic: giving her a single red rose every week for the longest time, singing and dancing at any opportunity, music always music, getting performers to play our song, countless larger live shows in the best seats, sneaking backstage, amazing evenings with people we met while travelling that we never saw again, but remembered fondly, wonderful sights and sounds, incredible meals, endless conversations, silliness and laughter, always laughter... Oh, we were in love and it seemed it would last forever. But that is an illusion and in what seems like the blink of an eye it can be gone, it can be too late...

The Short Answer...

So, what is love, and how can you find it and keep it alive? How many philosophers and individuals have tried to define love and who has ever really succeeded? We know it when we feel it, although often I think people are referring to infatuation or being "in love."

That feeling of being in love can be just an illusion if you don't make the right choices. And in what seems like the blink of an eye it can be gone, it can be too late...

How about finding love? You don't want to be looking in all the wrong places, which is what most people do. If you learn to choose wisely, something most people do not do, you will see how choosing someone mostly based on how you *feel* is a mistake.

The choice of a partner is the one point in time where you have the most control over how difficult or easy that relationship will be, the one time when you have the most control over your future. You may work harder later in the relationship, but it is in the choosing, in deciding whom to commit to, that you should invest the most care, energy and intelligence.

Are Both of You Good to Go?

If you are already in a committed relationship there are tools in this book to help you, but how hard you will have to work is already determined by the initial choice you have made. All of the advice in this book assumes that *both* people are willing to work together in a committed relationship. It only takes one person to end a relationship. It takes two to make it work. Choose wisely!

Finally, how do we keep love alive? How do we keep passion alive? How many times have you heard (or said) "I love him/her, I just don't feel *in love*," "We just fell out of love, grew apart," or "We have changed"?

Of course things change! Nothing stays the same. The more interesting question is, "How can you make better choices in what you do and how you think to keep the love alive?" All you need to know is 'how' and then apply that knowledge. You can make your relationship better and find the joy that love has to offer!

"It is not a lack of love, but a lack of friendship that makes unhappy marriages."
- Friedrich Nietzsche

Friendship starts at a minimum with trust, respect and affection. If you get those... that's pretty good. Finding a person with that same willingness to go further, and to fight to keep your love alive and vital is what this book is about. How do you find love and keep it alive? How do you keep the passion alive?

The answer... here it is in seven choices that you can make:

1. **Choose to love yourself.**

2. **Choose to take care of yourself.**

3. **Choose your partner and friends wisely.**

4. **Choose love and commitment every day.**

5. **Choose a structure for love.**

6. **Choose affection, sex and passion.**

7. **Choose humor, flexibility and spontaneity.**

These choices seem very simple. They are! However, the ideas need some explanation and elaboration to really make sense so that you can make these choices in a way that will make a difference in your relationship.

The essence of my thinking is here. Fully understand and make these seven choices, and you have no need to read further.

But I hope you will...

Love in the Beginning...

Ah, love! I admit it, I am a romantic. I have been goofy, silly and stupid at times when it comes to love, but I am getting much better at this. Of course, this is romantic love that I am referring to. Love is much broader than this, encompassing friendship, family, God, life, art, beauty and even pizza! You can probably think of spiritual moments, peak moments in nature or even experiences with music that led to transcendent feelings of appreciation and love of life. I hope you continue to have many of those moments! We love family and there is nothing like experiencing the love of a child or family member. We also love our pets and grieve them when they are gone... Given this complexity, I am limiting my focus here to romantic love between two people.

Travelling back in time, I keep slipping into memories of what we had... We are sipping bellinis in St. Mark's Square in Venice, listening to the dueling orchestras on a warm summer night in that ancient setting. It seems so decadent and we know we are the lucky ones, so in love. We know we have a great love and nothing can ever come between us...

Most of us would agree that love is definitely a powerful emotion, mostly pleasant and exciting, but also, at times, causing butterflies in the stomach and general feelings of anxiety. Influenced by thought, as we shall see below, love also influences (or maybe deranges!) our thoughts, contributing to obsessing about the person that later might become an ongoing concern for the person's well-being.

I like the partial definition of love offered in *The Road Less Traveled*, which implies the will to promote another's growth. This gives the notion of love a certain selfless responsibility for the other person. We want the loved one to grow, to be successful and truly happy, to achieve their goals, even if this means growing out of the relationship, leaving you behind. The actual quote is:

"Love is the will to extend one's self for the purpose of nurturing one's own or another's spiritual growth... Love is as love does. Love is an act of will -- namely, both an intention and an action. Will also implies choice. We do not have to love. We choose to love."

- M. Scott Peck, *The Road Less Traveled*

In my work with individuals in abusive relationships, I often use this quote to highlight how different this is from an abusive relationship, where the goal of the other person is to diminish their partner, to increase insecurity and to maintain control, often by any means necessary. Love is not selfish; it is our insecurity and fear that drive the selfishness and jealousy. We need to be courageous enough to dismiss those doubts, to have faith that we deserve love, are "okay" and can survive and find happiness again, even if the loved one leaves us.

An unusual description of love comes from an unlikely source:

"Only once in your life, I truly believe, you find someone who can completely turn your world around. You tell them things that you've never shared with another soul and they absorb everything you say and actually want to hear more. You share hopes for the future, dreams that will never come true, goals that were never achieved and the many disappointments life has thrown at you.

When something wonderful happens, you can't wait to tell them about it, knowing they will share in your excitement. They are not embarrassed to cry with you when you are hurting or laugh with you when you make a fool of yourself. Never do they hurt your feelings or make you feel like you are not good enough, but rather they build you up and show you the things about yourself that make you special and even beautiful.

There is never any pressure, jealousy or competition but only a quiet calmness when they are around. You can be yourself and not worry about what they will think of you because they love you for who you are. The things that seem insignificant to most people such as a note, song or walk become invaluable treasures kept safe in your heart to cherish forever.

Memories of your childhood come back and are so clear and vivid it's like being young again. Colors seem brighter and more brilliant. Laughter seems part of daily life where before it was infrequent or didn't exist at all. A phone call or two during the day helps to get you through a long day's work and always brings a smile to your face.

In their presence, there's no need for continuous conversation, but you find you're quite content in just having them nearby. Things that never interested you before become fascinating because you know they are important to this person who is so special to you. You think of this person on every occasion and in everything you do.

Simple things bring them to mind like a pale blue sky, gentle wind or even a storm cloud on the horizon. You open your heart knowing that there's a chance it may be broken one day and in opening your heart, you experience a love and joy that you never dreamed possible.

You find that being vulnerable is the only way to allow your heart to feel true pleasure that's so real it scares you. You find strength in knowing you have a true friend and possibly a soul mate who will remain loyal to the end. Life seems completely different, exciting and worthwhile. Your only hope and security is in knowing that they are a part of your life."

- Bob Marley

Taking Responsibility

In a healthy relationship, each person needs to be able to stand alone and take responsibility for his or her own happiness, recognizing their own needs and how to meet them. If one person in the relationship is overly needy from self-neglect or poor self-care, depressed or chronically in a bad place, this neediness pulls the relationship off balance. You need to meet as healthy equals, individually making sure that your needs for self-care are met.

All relationships go through difficult times and none of us is immune from getting depressed, anxious or fearful. It is wonderful to have someone to depend on for help through those times. However, if you are too often the rescuer or the one being rescued, something needs to change. In that will to promote your partner's growth can come the courage to insist upon better self-care, a change or some therapy to get back to that place of personal balance and well-being. In the next chapter, the first choice is discussed, loving yourself.

Choose to Love Yourself

It is a cliché that we must love ourselves before we can allow another to love us. That is because it is true! If you do not love yourself, how can you possibly let someone love you, or even let them close enough for this possibility to occur?

If you are convinced that you are "not okay" on some level, you are likely to keep others at a distance, rather than deal with the inevitable rejection that you are sure will occur when they discover the truth, that you are "not okay."

If by some chance you get past this and someone "rescues" you with their love, those lingering doubts can remain. Yes, it feels great to be with them and maybe this is what you needed to be able to love yourself? But you might wonder, maybe something is wrong with them? There must be if they think *you* are so wonderful, and you KNOW that you are actually "not okay."

Fast-forward down the road in the relationship... this often does not end well.

No Shortcuts

There is no shortcut. Do the work and self-exploration to learn to love yourself just the way you are. Yes, even YOU are loveable and wonderful, just the way you are. Sure, there might be some changes you want to make... If you are, for example, not a very nice person, you might commit to being nicer. I am convinced that the mean and angry people we run into are so mean because they have to deal with a horrible enemy – themselves! Whatever we see them dish out to the world pales next to how they treat themselves. In my professional life, I have dealt with lots of people like that, and it is amazing how much better they do when they learn to not take themselves and the world so seriously, and finally develop a sense of humor.

The really great thing about making changes for the better is that you do not have to complete the changes, you do not have to be perfect to be okay. You just have to commit to making *improvements* to those things that you don't like about yourself. Everyone likes a comeback story and we all have the chance to do this at any time. One small step at a time doing the right thing can feel wonderful. You might even decide that those things you hated about yourself are not so bad after all, that you are actually fine just the way you are. Only when you accept and love yourself are you open to letting others care about you. You are wonderful, and why wouldn't they think so too? Choose to love yourself!

Feelings Follow Thoughts

In trying to understand love, I end up using the tools I am most familiar with, and in my private practice of psychotherapy I often use a cognitive-behavioral model. I am not going to go into this in detail, but I find the concepts helpful. Being pragmatic, I like to use what works. Basically, the notion is that our feelings follow our thoughts; how we think influences or controls our feelings. It is often unrecognized irrational thinking or beliefs that lead to feeling anxious or depressed, and to low self-esteem. Part of the work mentioned above in learning to love yourself is to identify these thoughts and replace them with the truth: "I am okay."

When you first decide that someone in your life is possibly "meant for you," you begin the process of obsessing about that person (thinking) that leads to infatuation (feeling), something we often later describe as being "in love." No doubt love also has its roots in genetic factors, pheromones, hormones and early conditioning from our prior experiences. Enter the mostly pleasant physiological state of arousal. Enter sex or the possibility of sex. Positive fantasies and thoughts about that person, combined with at least some positive experiences when together, lead to more obsessing and stronger feelings of being in love.

Other feelings that can be very distressing complicate the picture: fear, nervousness, mania, joy, elation and excitement, to name a few. These are just part of the process of being "in love." They are influenced by your self-esteem, the appropriateness of the choice and the amount of perceived social and personal risk involved.

Much of the early part of any love relationship involves some fantasy because we really do not know the person all that well. We fill in the gaps based on our past experiences and expectations. At some point, reality crashes in as we gather information and reality – how the person really is and how we relate to each other in real life – conflicts with our expectations. This is a natural process that will repeat itself throughout the relationship and I will discuss this in detail later.

I can still clearly remember the night we met at a mutual friend's engagement party. My "wingman" and I are teasing her and she gives as good as she gets. Wow, she is so quick, so verbal. My wingman looks at me, nods and walks away. We go out on the patio and she sits with her lovely, long dark curls highlighted by a light behind her. I think to myself, "Oh man, you are in trouble now." I walk her to her car and we share one gentle kiss.

The next weekend we have an amazing first date at the beach in Laguna; everything is perfect. She later tells me that she went home that night and wrote in her journal that she is going to marry me. Two years later, it comes true...

The relationship seems easy and exciting when you are first in love, and it feels like it will last forever. This intensity does not last and, in fact, the feelings associated with being in love last on average for two years or less.

In the next phase, our naturally selfish natures can rise to the surface, and things can become much less pleasant. It is only your own decision to keep on loving, and behaving in a loving fashion, that can keep the love alive. If the relationship survives this, it may move on to a more stable period we might call "love" (as opposed to being "in love"). You may be happy to shed a little of the excitement for the comfort of a more stable way of relating and feeling. Those things which at first annoy you may become endearing or at least more tolerable as the relationship matures.

I was disappointed that she was not as neat and conscientious as I thought she would be. She would grab a can of soda, pour it in a glass, and then walk away leaving the can and a few drops of soda on the counter. Eventually she would clean it up, but why not do it right away when she poured it in the glass? I pointed out the logic of this but the behavior never changed.

I was reminded of the story of this man who came home from work every day and complained to his wife and kids about the toys left all over the yard. "I paid good money for those toys!" he would rant. One day, his wife and kids were killed in an automobile accident. When he returned home that day, he found the front yard to be neat, without the usual mess of toys. He cried as he realized how much he missed the mess...

I looked at the soda can and minor mess on the counter and smiled...

You certainly can see that love is a complicated thing. It is characterized initially by obsessive thinking about the loved one leading to intense arousal and feeling "in love." Later, if we are lucky and choose wisely, it can be experienced as a more stable concern and caring for the other person. It also involves responsibility for our own well-being and the will to promote the growth and well-being of the other person. It is a choice that you make and keep alive by what you do, how you think, and by the stories you choose to tell yourself and others about your love...

Choose Your Partner and Friends Wisely

The temptation when thinking about the process of choosing a partner is to wonder, "Did I make a good choice?" If you have made your choice and you are in a committed relationship, don't second guess yourself. You are committed! Use the strategies in this book to make your relationship stronger, better and more fulfilling. You already have love in your life and that makes you one of the lucky ones. Appreciate it and enjoy it and grow it!

If you are not committed, but dating someone, the information in this section can help you get clearer about the choices you make, and to make those choices in a thoughtful, more considered manner.

Many people have asked me how to find love and how to make a good choice when they are having difficulty finding love, after making bad choices again and again. These ideas can help you if you are struggling with this issue. These concepts also apply to choosing friends and so understanding these ideas will be time well spent.

Only at the Beginning Can we Change our Future

It is only at the beginning that you have the ability to make a choice that will determine just how much work your relationship will require.

Choose wisely! It is at this point that we should use the most intelligence, the most care. This may be the most important choice you ever make!

Unfortunately, most people choose a partner based on how it feels to be with that person, using their heart and not their head. What often feels good is what is familiar, but what if what is familiar is not a good thing? Suppose that you grew up in a family with an absent father and a critical mother. You just might be more comfortable around someone who is critical, which would eventually be a problem. Or you might be more comfortable with a person who is emotionally distant or emotionally unavailable, which would eventually be a problem. In both cases your needs for acceptance and love would not be met.

I believe that if you grew up in a household where your needs for acceptance and love were not met, you may struggle with low self-esteem and long for love and acceptance. You end up wanting to recreate the relationship that you had with your parent(s), but change the outcome to have a happy ending.

The problem is that if you choose someone who is selfish, critical and/or emotionally unavailable you will not get that happy ending. You cannot change another person! Oh sure, they might get hit by lightning or have an epiphany, or get a clue and change, but I wouldn't count on it!

To make love work long term, choose someone who does not need fixing, and who is already able to be a solid partner and deliver the love and acceptance you long for.

Are you following? This is the problem in choosing a partner based on how it feels, and this is just one example. I saw plenty of people in my practice who kept choosing partners who were abusive, or had alcohol problems, or who cheated on them time after time, because at the beginning of the relationship it "felt right," and the forces that pull you into that perfectly bad choice are powerful! It is an amazing process whereby we make those exquisite choices. Choose wisely!

The problem is using how it *feels* to be with that person as the end-all, the reason for choosing them. I think how it feels when you spend time together is important, and that is useful information, but that information is just some data that makes up a part of a much larger picture. I have a model for relationship choice that I have developed after seeing so many bad choices and helping individuals learn to make better choices.

Again, there is no shortcut. You must learn to love yourself and gain some insight into what your vulnerabilities are, understand which needs were not met during those important developmental years.

By the way, if you are one of those lucky souls who grew up in a loving family that purposely worked to support you and gave you lots of love and acceptance, it is much more likely that what *feels* right might in fact *be* right. But even given such ideal circumstances, I still think you should use your head instead of your feelings to make a better, more rational choice.

I was raised by wolves, I often quip, with almost no supervision during many critical periods of my development. I ran free and wild and I thank God that there were a few people who showed up in my life to keep me from straying too far... And then, during adolescence there were crushing, punishing attempts to control my behavior, failed attempts that led to open rebellion. This all contributed to my becoming a perfectionist, expecting too much of myself and others, struggling with self-esteem, control and anger. Again, amazing people showed up in my life who loved me and guided me, helped me to understand, gain insight and be a better person. I thank God that they were there for me. To this day, I am still a difficult person to deal with at times, but it could have been much worse. It is only my vigilance and commitment to love that give me a chance, and it is really no wonder that when I failed to be vigilant things fell apart...

So, how do you choose wisely? Choose mostly with your head and not entirely with your heart...

A Model for Relationship Choice

Start with a list of the characteristics that you would want and not want in a long-term relationship. Spend some serious time on this. Of course, many people already do this.

The next step is very important. Rate each item as negotiable or non-negotiable. Negotiable characteristics are just that, not essential. You might list things like attractiveness, ability to play certain sports, or likes reading and watching movies.

Non-negotiable problems are by definition characteristics that you would not tolerate in a long-term relationship, such as an alcohol or drug problem, extreme self-centeredness, anger problems, dishonesty, not being reliable, serious money problems or emotional or physical unavailability, to name but a few. (Should I mention texting while driving? Smart phone addiction?) This list could also include characteristics that must be present for a long-term relationship to work, such as honesty, fidelity, flexibility, a sense of humor, sexual compatibility and good communication skills.

Your relationship choice list is unique to you. Be clear about what you want and do not want. Now, keeping that information in mind, be a bit of a detective but don't make it obvious.

Take it Slow

I like the old-school idea of going slow at the beginning of a relationship to allow time to better see the person and to spot non-negotiable problems.

Once you become sexually or emotionally involved, it becomes much more difficult to be objective. With a greater level of emotional investment too soon, you may start to make excuses for how the person acts, or tell yourself that they will change later, ignoring the problem.

Listen to what they tell you, even if they pass it off as a joke. They are often telling you who they really are. "I'm so unreliable, ha, ha," or "I'm so disorganized," or "Sometimes you can't believe a word I say, ha, ha!" Listen and be curious, ask questions in an interested manner. Develop a clear picture of who this person is relative to your relationship choice list.

Got it? Here is the rule: once you have enough evidence that there is a non-negotiable problem, run, don't walk, for the exit! If you hang around long enough, you just might get sucked into that black hole known as the perfectly bad choice. Do not underestimate how powerful the forces and emotions can be that could pull you into that perfectly bad choice!

But it Feels Great

Let's look at how this might happen. You meet this person and it feels great when you're together. The person is very attractive, sex is great, and you have lots of common interests. You start to notice that they are pretty self-centered, that he or she is not happy if they don't get their way, that they lack empathy for the problems of others, although they hide it at first. Because you have a lot in common and because they are trying to please you (to get what they want), the self-centeredness does not lead to much conflict.

Remember that everyone is on good behavior at first and any problems that you observe during this phase are likely to be magnified later. Eventually, it really is going to bother you that he or she does not care what you want, and is only in it for what they can get.

Here is the catch: when will you come to that realization? After the emotional pull is so great that you make excuses for them, that you engage in denial that is hard to see through? After you are married? It will be much harder to get out then, and will take a greater emotional toll.

Wouldn't it have been better to realize this earlier and get out of the relationship before you were committed? Remember, it is only at the beginning when you are choosing a partner, that you have this much control over your future.

Realistically, you could have a long-term relationship with a wide range of individuals. At one end of this continuum it would take *A LOT* of work to continue the relationship. At the other end, it would take much less work. All relationships require some work. Whether the union requires a lot of work, or a little, or somewhere in between depends upon the choice you make. Choose wisely!

Choosing Friends

The same concepts apply to choosing friends. The people you surround yourself with will impact your marriage. Choose wisely and use your head. Choose friends without non-negotiable problems. Choose friends who don't need to be fixed before they are okay. Choose friends who are supportive of you and your marriage, and who share your interests and values. Don't be afraid to exclude people who threaten your marriage, and erect boundaries to protect your marriage and family when necessary.

Choose Love and Commitment Every Day

Okay, so you have made your choice and now you are committed to growing and keeping alive the love in your marriage. I am pulling for you! I am hoping that you have chosen wisely and get to reap the benefits of a good match. The best predictor of success for a couple is commitment. You and your partner must commit to working on the relationship and your love *every day*. The ideal is that every gesture and word reflect that love. That is an ideal, a goal. I recognize that we all are human and will fall short of this, but if we fall too short, if we neglect love, in the blink of an eye it can be over, it can be too late.

I hang my head in shame as I think of how badly I behaved at times when I was not being vigilant, not paying attention. Sure, we have both said mean things when angry, but I am responsible for my own behavior and that is the only thing I have control over. I could have done better, I should have done better, and I did not. Now we both pay the price for not recognizing how fragile love is, for not remaining vigilant in our commitment to love. Now, it is too late...

Appreciative Eyes

You and your partner must commit to continue to see each other with appreciative eyes, starting every day with a commitment to be kind, loving, understanding and patient. This also is a commitment to being present and *remaining* present in the relationship moment by moment. This is one of the most important choices that you both must make.

Responding vs. Reacting

Responding to each other rather than *reacting*, is one of the choices you can make as part of your commitment to the relationship. Responding is slower, it opens the communication and maintains the connection of your commitment. Reacting is quick, a knee-jerk reaction that is often defensive, leading to conflict.

She says, "I'm angry at what you just did!"

You *react*, "Hell, you've done worse!" and it's off to the races!

Better if instead, you pause for a moment and *respond*, "What was it I did that upset you?" or "How can I help you honey?"

The truth is, you never want to defend yourself with the person you love. It is far more important that you show your concern for your partner, your concern for why they are upset, rather than defending yourself, trying to prove your innocence.

Remember, there are two ways to start a fight: attack or defend. Either can start a fight! All couples have disagreements, but you don't have to be disagreeable.

You can learn to fight fair, where you both discuss the concerns without personal attacks. Remember that in a fair fight, you never hit below the belt. When you are angry it is possible to say things that may be very hard for the relationship to recover from. This must stop! Remain aware and vigilant enough to stay on track and do these simple things that protect your fragile love.

Choose to Take Care of Yourself

Again, in a healthy relationship, each person needs to be able to stand alone and take responsibility for his or her own happiness, recognizing their own needs and how to meet them. If one person in the relationship is overly needy from self-neglect or poor self-care, this neediness pulls the relationship off balance. You need to meet as healthy equals, individually making sure that your needs for self-care are met. These include eating well, getting enough sleep and exercise, and taking care of your emotional needs by balancing work, play, time alone and social support. I believe a sense of humor is essential, mostly because it is fun, but also because a sense of humor promotes flexibility, an essential tool in any relationship.

Basic Self-Care

I am surprised at how often I find individuals neglecting simple basic self-care. We all know that we must attend to our basic needs: eating well, getting enough sleep and exercise. Neglecting any of these increases stress, which makes communicating and relationships more difficult. You are much more likely to *react*. Good self-care keeps you in a better state of mind, making it more likely you will be able to *show up* and *respond*!

Social Support

Perhaps the best medicine for lowering stress and aiding your general well-being is social support. I define this as time with people who make you feel good, who validate you, who think you are wonderful. These are the people that help you to laugh and to be more appreciative of yourself and life. We all vary in terms of how much time we need with others, but we all can benefit from social support.

Balancing You, Me, and Us

Remember that you want to respect the needs of your relationship, to be aware of the needs and wants of your partner, and to show support for them in ways that they will appreciate. If you are unavailable to them because you spend too much time at work, out with friends, or alone, they will not feel supported.

Every relationship is different, and you must check in with each other frequently to confirm that you are maintaining the correct balance for your relationship. This is balancing the "you," the "me" and the "us." Too much time together and the relationship can stagnate. We all need some time apart to gain perspective, and often this helps you to appreciate each other more! Too much time alone or otherwise occupied and you have no relationship!

As a Psychologist I spend lots of time intensely involved with people, their thoughts, their feelings and their lives. As rewarding as this can be, it also is exhausting. By nature an introvert, I need lots of alone time to recharge my battery.

My wife was very supportive of this, including supporting my desire to spend time golfing, alone and with friends. We discussed this at length and she knew that I would be more attentive and more appreciative of her after some alone time.

We found a balance that worked for a long time, but gradually, slowly, we checked in less frequently and so we did not notice that we were out of balance. We did not pay attention to the increasing distance and dissatisfaction with our arrangement. By the time someone noticed, it was too late...

Don't make that same mistake, don't ignore your relationship! Pay attention, reach out and ask right now! Hug your partner and have the conversation, right now!

Choose A Structure for Love

There is an older couple that lives near me and I see them almost daily as they go about their lives. They have been married for 57 years, I discovered, and they still obviously enjoy each other's company. Each gesture, every look, every word reflects their love and friendship as I see them holding hands crossing the street, shopping and cooking dinner together at the communal barbeque.

I wanted that in my marriage. I still want that, and I will have something like that. So can you. So far, we have seen that you must take care of and learn to love yourself, choose wisely and commit to choosing love moment by moment.

So, what is the nature of the work? How do you keep love alive? The prerequisites listed above are essential, but I believe you need to choose to use more structure. You will do better with a common structure, when you both know what the rules are and commit to following them.

To ensure that you remain patient, respectful and appreciative of each other, develop a structure that will help you communicate effectively and include rules that you both follow.

Take a look at the context you want for your relationship. Love starts at a minimum with a deeply committed friendship. I often tease the couples I see that they would never treat their friends the way they treat each other because they would lose their friends. You should treat your partner as your best friend, with more care than anyone else in your life. Again, you must resist this very human tendency to take each other for granted, the common tendency to lash out in anger or frustration, to act badly.

The Benefit of the Doubt

Within this context, approach each other with patience and give each other the benefit of the doubt. The "benefit of the doubt" means trusting your partner's intentions, no matter how it feels or appears at the moment, even when they are acting badly. This involves trusting that if your partner could see how the behavior is affecting you, and they knew a better way to behave, they would do it. You need to trust that the reason they are not behaving better is because they are confused, or distracted, or having an emotional problem. They could be tired, or hungry, or stressed out or just plain inept. Giving him or her the benefit of the doubt just might give you the patience to gently call them on their behavior and suggest returning to the issue later when you might have a more productive discussion about it. Be patient with yourself and your partner. Patience is a very loving act.

When in doubt, slow down the communication. Take a break and come back to it when you can both respond and not react. Remember, you are more likely to be reactive when you are hungry, tired, stressed out, distracted, impatient or in a hurry to get somewhere. These are not the times to discuss something that is important! If even one of you can spot this you can stop and reschedule a time to continue the discussion. If now is not the right time to talk, for one or both of you, remember to schedule a *specific* time to get back to it. This supports your faith that you will resolve the issue, just not right now.

The Team Meeting

Schedule a meeting to talk ahead of time. Even if your partner agrees to talk when you spring an issue on them, you will do better to have time to get your heads in the right place and remember the context for effective communication, remembering that you are partners on the same side, giving each other the benefit of the doubt, and reviewing the strategies for good communication. Limit the scheduled discussion to 45 minutes or less and keep to one issue.

Don't indulge in late-night marathons! The suggestion to never go to bed angry does not mean that the issue must be *resolved* before going to bed. It simply means that you must agree to set it aside until later, have faith that you will solve it then, and be nice to each other in the meantime.

Use a structure for the meeting and follow the rules of a communication model. I like the idea of the meeting as a sandwich, with the beginning and the end (the bread) focused on what is going well in the relationship, and the meat or middle of the session focused on the issue at hand. Beginning your discussion by talking about what is working makes it more likely that you will continue to do those things. Reward success! Reward is much more powerful than punishment. You want to make sure that your relationship has an abundance of rewards!

Phrase requests positively and always ask for more of something. Which request would you rather hear: "You never take me anywhere!" or "Let's go out and do something fun together, shall we dear?"

Reflective Listening

Use a strategy called *reflective listening*. You have probably already heard of this or used it in another context. The variation of reflective listening I like to use goes like this: Your partner starts out by introducing the topic and concern, and then you summarize what they say using three stages to make sure *you* understand the message, and to let *them* know you understand the message.

The first stage is to summarize the *content* of the message, often using your partner's words. After it is agreed that you understand the content, you summarize what you think is *meant* by the message, the *meaning*. Finally, when it is agreed that you understand the meaning, you move on to *validation*. This simply involves acknowledging your partner's point of view, that it makes sense, that they are not crazy for having that belief, even if you disagree.

At this point you have *objectivity*, which is knowing that you are talking about the same thing, and you may respond back to your partner, *on topic*. Objectivity is such a rare thing. How many times have you seen a discussion go on and on before you realized that you were talking about different things?

After establishing objectivity, you *respond* and your partner goes through the three stages, summarizing what you just said, *content, meaning* and *validation*, and so on. This is very slow and awkward at first, but becomes easier as you practice and make the model your own. Although awkward, this structure can help you avoid countless problems that can occur in a rapid-fire, impatient conversations or arguments.

Take some time right now if you can to practice this together. Re-read the section. Practice giving each other compliments, using the communication model to practice reflective listening.

And now, here is a life-long assignment: watch your partner for things that they do that you like, and compliment them on those things, reward them for doing nice things! They are more likely to do those things in the future and it helps you both to continue seeing each other with *appreciative eyes*.

This model really is only for use for important issues in a meeting that you have scheduled ahead of time; you will make yourself and those around you nuts if you talk like this during everyday conversations! Be patient. When in doubt, slow down. Remember that approximately 70% of communication (and maybe much more) is non-verbal, and be aware of how you say things. Your tone of voice, facial expressions and gestures are all important. The music is more important than the words! The goal is not to convince your partner of anything; the goal is to try and understand each other. Two people impatiently trying to convince each other is an argument. Two people patiently trying to understand each other have a much better chance of doing just that! Clarity is more important than agreement.

Communicating in the Moment

Sometimes you just need to talk *right now* because you want some support, or you need to discuss an everyday issue that does not warrant a "team meeting." For more informal discussions, I have a suggestion. If you are the one initiating the discussion, *let the other person know what their role should be.*

For example, you could say, "Please just listen and don't say anything," or "Listen and tell me how wonderful I am and how much the other guys suck!" You could ask the other person to just hold you while you talk. The important thing is that you get exactly what you want from the other person, and they don't have to guess, which can be a problem when they guess wrong.

Making Decisions Together

Take a moment to consider how you make decisions together. I saw a young couple who argued about buying a jet ski. He really wanted that jet ski and pressured her at every opportunity. She, very reasonably, pointed out that the purchase did not fit in their budget. He continued to pressure her until she finally, unhappily agreed. She then would get angry every time he went out on the jet ski. He discovered that he did not enjoy the jet ski as much as he thought he would. Every time he went out he felt guilty about how he had pressured her.

How you treat each other while you are making a decision, and that you are both okay with the decision, are more important than the decision.

Read that again! The relationship is always more important than the task! How you treat each other is what matters. You never want to get your way at the other's expense, because of the damaging effect this can have on your relationship. You can pay now, or you can pay later!

So, you can see that this commitment made every day is actually a moment-by-moment

choice to have a loving partnership and friendship, a commitment to patient and respectful communication, to responding and not reacting, and to giving each other the benefit of the doubt. It is a choice to focus on understanding and clarity rather than making a point or trying to get your way, a choice to be aware of and responsible for your non-verbal communication, choosing so that every word and gesture reflect your love.

Choose Humor, Flexibility and Spontaneity

Now here comes an inconsistency in this little book (after all, if you don't have to struggle a bit with these ideas, you are not truly engaged with the choices outlined in this book!) Despite my talking about being committed to your relationship and working on making it as good as it can be every moment, you must recognize that this is an impossible task!

Just Enjoy Each Other Most of the Time

I believe that you should spend a *small* amount of time *working* on the relationship, and *most* of your time just *enjoying* each other. The moment-by-moment awareness of your love and remembering to remain loving are essential, but the trick is to make them into habits. No one can *work* constantly on a relationship. Being kind and loving is not that hard to do with the kind of commitment I have been discussing, but *working* on the relationship can be exhausting.

Be flexible, look for humor and opportunities to laugh, and allow for spontaneity. It can be great fun to enjoy the naturally occurring opportunities to laugh about how silly we all can be at times.

So, most of the time you should be just enjoying each other, and as you notice issues that need to be addressed you can schedule team meetings as needed. I like to encourage routine team meetings, for example weekly, to check in with each other to make sure both of you are getting your needs met and to keep rewarding what is working.

If you have children you, or they, can schedule "family meetings." This gives your kids the opportunity to address really important issues like allowances or daily chores, and they get to learn about effective and positive communication.

This is a chance to confirm that you are each providing the words or actions that matter most to each of you. In other words; are you being supportive enough so that you both feel loved and valued. Support is defined by the receiver, not the giver. What makes you feel loved may not be perceived as support by your partner. She may love compliments, while you couldn't care less about compliments, as long as you get lots of affection and/or sex.

For one couple, it became clear that she loved back rubs above all else. Wanting to please her husband, she gave him the experience she craved. She had him lie down while she got out lightly scented oil and massaged his whole back, taking care to rub all the areas that she loved getting rubbed.

He said, "Yeah, that's nice dear."

But inside, he was silently screaming, "You're touching the wrong side!"

Don't assume that your partner will like the same kinds of support that you like. We each have specific wants and needs. Talk about and learn the things that make each of you feel supported and loved.

Gary Chapman does an exceptional job of describing the different ways we might show our love and support to our partners. In his amazing book, **"The 5 Love Languages,"** he describes five methods for expressing or receiving love and support, his five love languages. These are: **words of affirmation, quality time, receiving gifts, acts of service, and physical touch.** If you have not read this book *, read it! You want to be sure to put your energies into the correct activities to show your love and support for each other. (* The 5 Love Languages, by Gary Chapman, 1992, Northfield Publishing).

If you are not feeling loved and supported, and this is not discussed, resentments can build. Don't let dissatisfactions go without resolution! If you do they can fester and create resentment. I have seen again and again the intrusive and destructive force of an unresolved problem intruding on a constant basis. You must learn to set problems aside, continue to enjoy each other, and trust that you *will* develop a solution to any problems you may have during your scheduled team meetings.

Let me clarify with an example. At one time or another most couples experience some difficulties in their sexual relationship, such as a disagreement about frequency. This may actually reflect an underlying loss of desire, the most common sexual difficulty, and I address this a little later in the book. The problem becomes bigger when one or both of you feel the pressure of the problem all of the time, or refer to it frequently, or give each other the cold shoulder. No cold shoulders! This is not a loving way to behave!

So, I suggest giving a more proportional amount of time to the work, reflecting the proportion of your relationship that the activity represents. Even if you are having sex like bunny rabbits, you are still probably spending less than three percent of your time engaged in sex! So, how could you let this problem dominate *all* of your waking hours? It is much more rational to save dealing with the problem, whatever it is, within the confines of the team meeting.

During the rest of the time, have faith that you will resolve the issue just like you have every other problem. Respect this boundary and be nice to each other in between! This use of trust and the ability to set problems aside until the appropriate time is something that must be built into the structure that holds your relationship together, that helps you keep the love alive.

You will find that issues come up that must be dealt with right then, and life must go on, as it should! You will be having a conversation, or even a team meeting, when suddenly emotions escalate and the talking becomes unproductive (Grrr!). Call "time out," which means that you both stop talking, go into your respective corners to cool off for a moment, come back and hug it out. Then schedule a team meeting to deal with that discrete issue at the next opportunity. Forcing the discussion right then, when you are both upset and *reacting*, will not be productive! Even a short break to cool down and gain perspective can be very helpful.

Between now and the team meeting, continue to be nice to each other, even if you are really angry about the issue. (Grrr!) Have the *faith* to trust that you will resolve the issue in that meeting or in subsequent meetings. Sometimes it takes multiple meetings to work through an issue, with time in between to think about what was discussed.

This use of *time out* and having faith in each other is something you must learn to do. It is one of the many choices you can make to strengthen your commitment to each other.

Three Phases of Growth

I think of growth in a relationship as a three-phase cycle: joy, disillusionment, and working through. Joy is easy! Let's have lots of that! Inevitably you will become disappointed or disillusioned with some part of the relationship. This is not an excuse to withdraw or get angry, it is a necessary part of growing together! It is a reminder that you have some work to do, some things to work through to get back to joy.

This three-phase process affects all of your relationships, including with yourself, your job, and even your car!

When that car was new you really loved it! Over time, it got older and less shiny and the new car smell went away. You might have become disillusioned with the car and started noticing those newer models out there. Then you remembered that this is a familiar process and that all you needed to do was figure out what *working through* was needed to get back to the joy of that relationship with your car.

You took the car in and had it tuned up, bought new tires and rims, got it detailed and added some "new car" scent. Not bad! No one could convince you to trade that car in. You love it!

Do the work. Enjoy the time in between. Be patient with yourself and each other.

An important part of the joy in your relationship is time spent out on dates. Planning and looking forward to fun events helps to keep the connection alive. I was always a fan of tracking and finding live music events and festivals, but you can pursue a wide variety of activities that help to keep the relationship exciting.

I have often heard couples complain that they "never" (by the way, never say "never"!) do anything new or exciting anymore. Looking at this issue I have to agree that many couples get stuck in ruts when it comes to dating. They end up only pursuing those activities that they know they *both* enjoy, and don't take risks with new activities. Dinner and a movie every week can get old. It's fun to try something new.

Taking Turns

One of my favorite suggestions is for you to build in **taking turns** dates. Not all the time, but once every month or so introduce a "taking turns" date.

Here are the rules for **when it is your turn**:

> 1.   You selfishly choose the activity for the two of you to do on a date
> 2.   You pay for the date and provide transportation
> 3.   You either tell your partner where you are going or, my favorite, you keep it a surprise and let them know what to wear so that they are dressed appropriately for the event, and
> 4.   You do your best to help them enjoy the date and attend to their comfort and safety.

When it is not your turn, your task is to **stay interested**. You are not allowed to complain and must try to make the best of the situation. Remember, next time it will be your turn and you get to selfishly decide what the date will be!

Most couples find that they enjoy discovering new activities and the rules make it much more likely that you will have a good time. Remember that the goal is to have fun and *not* to make your partner suffer, so don't choose activities that you know would frighten or seriously upset your partner. I love planning a new activity as a surprise, and who doesn't like a pleasant surprise?

Again, this is about introducing more fun into your relationship! Remember fun? I discuss this later, but happiness starts with being thankful... Keep seeing each other with *appreciative eyes*, be flexible, look for humor and opportunities to laugh, and allow for spontaneity. It can be great fun to be "goofy" together and enjoy the naturally occurring opportunities to laugh about how silly we all can be at times.

If this is hard for you, I prescribe that you watch 30 minutes of comedy each day. Find something that really makes you laugh and get your daily dose of this. You will find that you see more humor around you in your daily life as long as you remember to "show up" and pay attention to the vital and immediate life pulsing around you.

Choose Affection, Sex and Passion

So, you have been reading about commitment, communication and the structure that I believe makes for a better relationship, and you happily notice that you are already doing much of what I suggested with good results. Yes! I am pulling for you and the success of your love! Ain't love grand! If sex is great too, then you are living the dream! Even so, at some point you may benefit from some helpful ideas in this area.

If you are having trouble in this area, don't ignore it or let it deteriorate further. I heard about one couple where it had become so bad that their most frequent position was "doggie style." No! Not that! It was where he was down on all fours begging for sex, and she rolled over and played dead... Seriously, you can do better than this.

Better Sex

If sex is not all you would like it to be, you can make it better. You have been making good choices, finding solutions and growing your love. You can make this area great too! You are great friends and partners, you enjoy each other and maybe friends comment on how great your marriage seems. It is a great marriage! But it's possible that you have let sex and passion become lower priorities, or maybe you have never fully explored these aspects of your relationship.

Many couples have trouble talking about sex. Sex is often easier done than said! Remember that you have a good relationship, you can talk to each other and you are committed to each other. You can make your relationship more passionate. Together you can make your marriage whatever you want it to be!

Guidelines for Good Sex

Making this better will be easier than you think if you commit to growing this part of your marriage. There are some practical issues to attend to:

1) finding time for intimacy and sex,

2) addressing any fears, misunderstandings or knowledge deficits,

3) establishing a pace and frequency that is comfortable for both of you,

4) communicating about preferences in an open manner before, during and after sex, and

5) keeping humor and fun alive in all aspects of your relationship.

Whatever your position is on the issue of size, remember that the largest sex organ is the brain! The most important part of making a difference takes place between your ears. It is learning to look at your partner with appreciative eyes.

This also is about showing up and engaging your partner, not allowing yourself to be distracted by the internet and smart phones. I recently saw a quote that stated that 10% of people actually look at their smart phones at some time during sex! Another 35% check their phones immediately after sex! I have just three words to say about that: "That ain't right!" These habits distract us and can get in the way of human connection. Please remember my central message... If you stop paying attention, before you know it, it can be too late...

Let's take a look at human nature. We tend to appreciate newness, but it is not long before we take things for granted. When you first got together with your partner, you most likely began to obsess about him or her in a very positive manner.

"He is so handsome!"

"She is so hot!"

"I can't believe how considerate he was last night."

Since our feelings follow our thoughts, the feelings that follow such thinking are very pleasant! At first, we talk about infatuation that later is referred to as feeling "in love."

Over time, we tend to take these things for granted and our thoughts shift to the things that the other person does that irritate us.

"I really wish he could remember to put the toilet seat down, take out the trash, and pay more attention to my feelings."

"You would think she could remember to follow through with the things I ask her to do and stop nagging me. How could she forget to pay that #$!@ bill!"

Needless to say, the feelings that follow this kind of thinking are much less pleasant.

I often hear, "I still love him/her, but I'm not in love."

Being in love is a choice! To keep the feelings alive, you must interrupt the tendency to take things for granted and continue to see your spouse with appreciative eyes.

Give it a try. During the day, think about your spouse in an appreciative way.

Think about the nice things they have done and the things you like about them.

Dwell on these positive attributes and overlook or be more generous about their shortcomings (remember – they put up with your less-than-desirable characteristics also!)

That evening, when you first see each other again, you will notice the return of affectionate feelings. How strong those feelings are is largely up to you.

Your Love Story

Choose "the story" about your marriage carefully. We all tell ourselves stories about the various areas of our lives as part of making sense of our world and our lives. You are asked about your job or your relationship and you tell the story you have chosen about those areas. You may forget that it is just a story and confuse it with reality.

There are probably a hundred stories you could tell about any given situation, and none would capture the whole picture accurately. Some stories are more helpful, and some are destructive.

Choose wisely! If your story about your love relationship involves some version of "the old ball and chain" you may be causing damage to the relationship, even if you think it is funny.

Our sexual feelings operate in much the same way. Remember that sex is an appetite and can be influenced in a manner similar to our desire for food. The most common sexual dysfunction is loss of desire, and the way this happens is the same for most people.

At first sex can be very intense and the desire for sex can be very powerful, because at first it is new, and you obsess about sex and your partner's desirable characteristics!

Over time the newness wears off, and you begin to turn yourself off by thinking about the things that bother you about your partner. You don't do this on purpose. It is that natural human tendency to take things for granted. Living together you see each other on the toilet, in the morning with bad breath and no make-up, and at your worst in arguments. No wonder you don't want to have sex with that person!

The same solution can help us here. Continue to see your partner with appreciative eyes and fantasize about them during the day. Think about having sex and what you would like to give and to receive. You will notice an increase in desire when you are together.

The return of desire will be assisted greatly if you can let go of past resentments and continue to view your spouse in an appreciative sexual manner, when you are together and when you are apart. For you men (and some of you women), remember that "foreplay" is not what happen 30 minutes before intercourse. It is how you have been treating your partner for the previous week or month! Be nice!

Do not argue in bed and don't work in the bedroom. The bed should only be used for sleep and play. If you stick to this rule, the bed will always be a pleasant place to escape to.

For you women (and some of you men), desire is a funny thing and may not operate as you think. I saw a woman in my practice with her husband. Neither of them were having as much sex as they wanted, although they thoroughly enjoyed sex when they had it. Eventually it came out that she was waiting to be "in the mood" before seeking or agreeing to have sex, even though she was often open to the idea. On those occasions, she was encouraged to allow some physical stimulation to see if this influenced her "mood." It did, and this couple reported later that they were much more satisfied with their sex life. Research now suggests that as long as you are not opposed to it, allowing some stimulation can greatly increase desire and frequency.

Remain flexible and try new things. Keep the dialogue open and talk to each about what you want. I saw older couples who could not have intercourse because of medical problems, and who described having a very satisfying sex life. I have worked with individuals with spinal cord injuries with loss of sensation to their genitals, and who also found ways to have a satisfying sex life. If these people can do it, certainly you can!

There are many books about improving sex, and psychologists to help you if you are struggling in any of these areas. Don't be afraid to reach out for help. You will only regret it if you don't reach out before it is too late...

Separate Sex and Affection

I believe that you should keep affection and sex separate.

"What?!" you may ask.

That's right. Many couples I have seen use increased affection as a cue to initiate sex. Although this is nice, I think it can be a mistake. Everyone has times when they don't feel like having sex, and if affection is how you initiate sex you may avoid affection at those times to avoid initiating sex, even if you would have liked to hug and kiss and be held! This can be avoided by keeping them separate.

I encourage lots of affection. If you say you are not a hugger, you can learn to be one! Perhaps, at first, you are giving hugs because you have learned that your partner values hugs. That's fine as a start and is a loving act. Anyone can learn to get comfortable with hugs with enough practice. Here is a little tip for you; the key to enjoying a hug is to relax into it. Get up right now and hug your partner!

I recommend lots of affection on a regular basis while using another cue to initiate sex. One couple I saw would initiate sex with the question, "Would you like to hear a bedtime story?"

Initiating sex can be a simple direct or indirect question, or a cue that you both agree on. One couple I saw just could not talk about *sex*, and so they worked out a strategy of turning a statue on the fireplace mantle; if their partner turned it the rest of the way, they knew they were on! In this way, you never sacrifice affection to the confusion sometimes associated with sex.

While I'm discussing affection, I think it's important to talk about kissing. That's right, k-i-s-s-i-n-g! Remember when you were first dating, how wonderful and exciting kissing was? The thrill of that first kiss and all of the promise that it represented... oh yeah! Fast forward to today and I see lots of couples kissing much less after they have been together for awhile. You could change that if you like. You could choose to find more time for kissing. Keep your breath fresh so that you are ready if the opportunity presents itself. Look for opportunities to just sit together and kiss. Keep the romance alive!

Now, go hug and kiss your partner right now!

Love Lost and Found...

If you have been paying attention (and I hope you have because I'm pulling for you), then you have acquired some skills, some new ways to think about relationships, love, sex and life. I hope so! I am pulling for you and I want you to be happy! If you are happier, your life and love relationships will be easier and more satisfying.

Choose Happiness

I want to be sure that you know *how* to be happier! I believe that happiness starts with being thankful. Simply turn on your senses and appreciate what you see, hear, taste and touch.

In my work with people who are depressed and people who are happy, I have noticed that happiness really comes down to another moment-by-moment decision. Unhappy people are focused on loss or what is missing. Happy people choose to appreciate what is there. They are thankful for what is in their lives. Happiness is a choice and you are in control!

"There are only two ways to live your life. One is as though nothing is a miracle. The other is as though everything is a miracle."
- Albert Einstein

What are you doing moment-by-moment? Are you complaining and focused on what is missing, or are you thankful for what is there? If you are unhappy, shift focus to appreciate what is there, including your partner. Unhappy people misuse selective attention and focus on loss, on what is missing. If criticized, they dwell on this. If complimented, they dismiss it and give it little attention. If this is you, shift focus, shift attention, use your selective attention to support your happiness. Appreciate what is there and dwell on successes and compliments. When you make a mistake or are criticized, take away the lesson learned and move on, don't dwell on it!

Like love, happiness is a choice and life is too short to not figure out how to be happy!

"When I started counting my blessings my whole life turned around."
- Willie Nelson

Appreciate your partner, say, "Thank you!" Gratitude means the grass is greener right here! If you express gratitude, if you simply say, "Thank you," the other person will want to know more about you, will want to spend more time with you.

"The deepest craving of human nature is the need to be appreciated."
- William James

Despite all of your efforts, your knowledge and your commitment, you will make mistakes. You will screw up. Welcome to the human race! For these times, I would like to suggest two strategies:

Re-writing the interaction (the do-over)
Explicitly asking for forgiveness

The Do-Over

You may have had the experience of coming home, walking in the door and then either saying the wrong thing or overreacting to what was said... WHAM! Instant argument! Worse, the whole evening is ruined! Even if you both move on from that initial negative moment, the atmosphere can be tense.

This is where you say, "Hey honey, let's re-write the interaction." Some couples call this a do-over.

You go back out the door, and then come back in, "Hi honey, I'm home!" Now you get a second chance and can do a much better job, saving the evening.

You can do this anytime, anywhere, when you realize that you would like a chance to have a better interaction. It also reminds us that we all are trying to improve; we are all practicing.

Ask for Forgiveness

Sometimes when you ask for a do-over, your partner might say, "No! I'm still mad at what you said!" This is the time to explicitly ask for forgiveness, "Can you forgive me?"

If asked, and you choose to forgive, that means you let the issue go and don't bring it up again.

Before you forgive, maybe you want to have a discussion, or hear an apology. That is perfectly fine. Whatever it takes, moving to forgiveness is a wonderful thing. It gives you a fresh start, a clean slate, and we can all use a second chance sometimes. Practice explicit, genuine forgiveness with each other.

Like love and patience, forgiveness is a wonderful gift that you can give each other.

Lasting Love...

At the beginning of the book, I told you that it would be short. I prefer to think of it as small but mighty!

Thank you for taking the time to read this little book. Thank you for wanting to be a more loving human being. By using these simple ideas, I believe you will have deeper, more intimate, more loving and committed relationships.

So here you are, and here are the seven choices that you can make to find love and save your marriage, before it is too late:

1. **Choose to love yourself**

2. **Choose to take care of yourself**

3. **Choose your partner and friends wisely**

4. **Choose love and commitment every day**

5. **Choose a structure for love**

6. **Choose affection, sex and passion**

7. **Choose humor, flexibility and spontaneity**

Does this list of choices look different now? I hope so! I hope you see different and deeper meaning in these simple choices than you did before reading this book.

Of course, there are many more steps involved, but the important ideas are simple ones and I hope that they help you to be courageous and to take a chance on love. Love is right here, in your life for you to discover. Remember, as you look at each other with appreciative eyes, look for opportunities to express your love...

You know, life in general and my life in particular are not so bad. I am thankful for the people in my life, for the career that gives me so much opportunity to give back, and for being able to live in Hawai'i, such a beautiful place.

As I finish this little book, I can happily tell you that I have found love again... and so can you! Without a doubt, unequivocally, absolutely, I can say that love is the best of all that life has to offer...

About the Author

Originally from Southern California, Dr. Stephen Openshaw received his Masters and Doctorate in Clinical Psychology from Purdue University in Indiana. His dissertation was a study of telephone crisis intervention at the Los Angeles Suicide Prevention Center, one of the first crisis centers in the nation. During his internship, he focused on working with medical patient populations, in newly developing areas of Health Psychology called Consultation and Liaison, and Behavioral Medicine. He helped military veterans with spinal cord injuries and other serious injuries requiring rehabilitation. He also focused on working with couples, and received extensive training in couples therapy. He worked with one of the founders of the UCLA Human Sexuality Program, at the Institute for Sex and Marital Therapy, learning to help couples with their intimate difficulties.

Before moving to Hawai'i, he practiced as a Clinical Psychologist in Fullerton, California. He continued to work with couples and had a general psychotherapy practice for many years. In his hospital work, he continued to work with people struggling with spinal cord injuries, cardiac problems, and other acute or chronic medical conditions. He was actively involved in various roles with St. Jude Medical Center in Fullerton for 30 years, and was a member of the Medical Staff until 2013. After moving to Hawai'i, he worked as a counselor embedded in various Marine Battalions for a year at a time, including infantry, artillery and intelligence battalions.

To this day, he has always maintained that his greatest satisfaction remains the success he has had working with couples...

Dr. Openshaw lives happily in Hawai'i and continues to support our armed services as a Clinical Psychologist. Watch for the second book in the 7 Choices Series due out next year, "Seven Choices for Great Relationships in the Military."

Acknowledgments

Writing this book has proved to be great therapy for me, a cathartic process. Born out of pain, it has become a labor of love and, I hope, a gift of love to those who need some guidance. I am thankful for the family, friends, colleagues, and supervisors who have been there and helped me over the years.

Thank you to my brothers, Jeff, John and Ron, and my sister, Jennifer.

Thanks to Marion Buckmaster, Virginia Cooper, all of the Kennys, Kay Coleman, Christine Benavides, Lee Bradley, Dr. Pete Ebersole, Dr. Don Hartsough, Dr. Chris DeGraff, Dr. Doug Nitta, Dr. Ken Kaisch, and Dr. Lyn Dahlquist.

Thanks to Katie Coates for endless editing support, the book cover, and so much more.

Thank you to Colonel Ron Ells, Barbara Gosselin, Jennifer Openshaw, Jeff Openshaw, and anonymous (you know who you are!) for editorial assistance and support.

Thank You

Thank you for reading my little book. Please take the time to review this book on Amazon.com. I welcome your comments and criticism. You can help me make this a better book! It is a work in progress and if you spot a typo, have a suggestion or have an opinion, please email me at Author@OpenshawPhD.com. I can upload changes or improvements to the Kindle version of this book within 24 hours. Thank you for helping me to be a better writer! Feel free to share this book with your friends and family. Wishing you great success in your relationships!

71036854R00044

Made in the USA
Middletown, DE
19 April 2018